WELSH DIALECT

A selection of words and anecdotes
from around Wales

by
Benjamin A Jones

BRADWELL
BOOKS

Published by Bradwell Books
9 Orgreave Close Sheffield S13 9NP Email:
books@bradwellbooks.co.uk

British Library Cataloguing in Publication Data:
a catalogue record for this book is available from
the British Library.

1st Edition

ISBN: 9781910551653

Print: Gomer Press, Llandysul, Ceredigion SA44 4JL

Typeset by: Andrew Caffrey

Image Credits: iStock, Alamy Images, National Library
of Wales, and Richard Burton Archives.
Other images credited separately.

WELSH ENGLISH
DIALECT

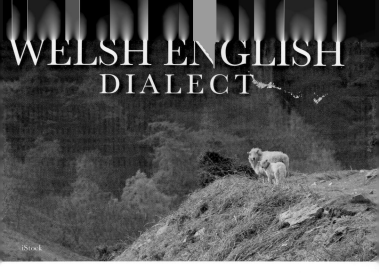

iStock

MUCH HAS BEEN WRITTEN about Wales's English dialects in the past, and the country has been subject to several dialect glossaries, often with a focus on the South Welsh valleys. The aim of this book, however, is to expand upon these glossaries, to not only include the lingo of the beloved valleys, but also to include English words from across Wales as well as from all walks of life, past and present. These include mining and farming words, as well as the language of children's games and well-known phrases. This book is not only a glossary of Welsh English dialects but also of English terminology used in Wales and Welsh culture, from Welsh cuisine to cultural traditions. Along with the dictionary, this volume aims to shed light on some traditions from Wales that you may not have read about. Perhaps you weren't aware of the names of traditional medieval Welsh instruments, or maybe you've been perplexed by the original naming method for Welsh children?

Many of these cultural *bara-bits* may, understandably, be of Welsh-language origin (English throughout Wales is a relatively new phenomenon), but today they are commonly used with pride by English speakers living in Wales too. In fact, there are some terms from that glorious Celtic language which are quite untranslatable, and have entered Welsh English as 'loan words'.

This book is a celebration of the way the English language is used in Wales in 2016. Its intention isn't academic, but its subject should be thought-provoking to all. The words you find in this book are words that have been genuinely recorded at some point from speakers, either recently or from the near past. Previous glossaries, poems and academic surveys have been scoured to provide a brief, but wholesome, picture of the way English has been used in Wales. Every effort has been made to obtain distinctly unique words from Wales. I have therefore endeavoured to leave out colloquial speech which may be spoken in other areas of the UK which may be found in other popular glossaries in the Bradwell Dialect series. This is a small volume, though, so if a dialectal word or subject you love hasn't made it in, please don't feel like it's any less important than entries that have!

Old map of South Wales iStock

Dialect areas

Contrary to popular belief, there's more than just one English dialect in Wales. Words unique to certain areas we've noted with letters.

Welsh Valleys English (Glamorgan) - *(V)*

The most recognised Welsh English. It has the largest population of speakers, and is often heard in television and film. Stretching from coastal Swansea to mountainous Blaenavon, it varies slightly between the valleys. The cities of the Severn Estuary, such as Cardiff and Newport, have similar vocabularies to Valleys English, but their pronunciations differ notably.

'Gowerland' English and 'Little England' English (Gower peninsula and South Pembrokeshire) - *(G)* and *(P)*

Unique words hail from this area, sharing little similarity with the Welsh-derived words found elsewhere. As Gower, South Pembrokeshire and parts of south Carmarthenshire (those below the 'Landsker Line') were within the historical Welsh Marches, they were colonised by English speakers far earlier (as early as the 12th century). The area was colloquially known as *'Little England Beyond Wales'* or *'Anglia Transwalliana'*. English influence came also from Cornwall and Devon via trade within the Bristol Channel. Perhaps most surprising is that within this dialect are several words of Scandinavian and Flemish origin, due to possible Viking settlement in the 9th and 10th centuries, followed later by Flemish settlers during the Norman invasion of Britain.

Border Welsh English (Powys, Monmouthshire) - *(B)*

The Welsh borders were some of the first areas of Wales to be anglicised (after the southern coasts) and therefore there are many unique English words along the border that have an established history. Several words and pronunciations have similar qualities to those used in nearby Herefordshire, Gloucestershire and Shropshire, but this region still retains many unique expressions of its own, especially anglicised loanwords from Welsh.

West Welsh English (Dyfed) and North Welsh English (Gwynedd & Clwyd) - *(W)* and *(N)*

Welsh is spoken largely in these areas. English usage tends to be quite standardised as it's often a secondary language. That doesn't mean there aren't unique words – there are: some Welsh, and some with perfectly English origins that may not be used further south. Unfortunately, these dialects often get neglected by popular glossaries. It should also be noted that the accents in the north-east are reminiscent of nearby Liverpool.

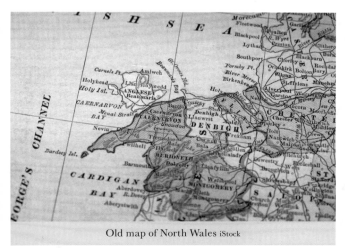

Old map of North Wales iStock

A

Ach-y-fi (ach) – Expression of disgust

Afanc/Avanc – Lake monster in Welsh folklore

All jaw – Variation on *'All mouth and no trousers'* *(V)*

Alleys – Game of marbles *(V)*

Anch (granch/hanch) – To bite. *'He anched the apple.'*

Angin' – Literally 'hanging' – unattractive or disgusting *(V/B)*

Anglo-Welsh – Half English, half Welsh

Arbed – To prevent or avoid, from Welsh *'I used a cloth to arbed making a mess'* *(W)*

Arsey – Annoyed *(B)*

Askel – Newt

B

Bach – Term of endearment, literally 'small' in Welsh (male) (cf. *fach*) *(V)*

Badly off – Opposite of *'well off'* (i.e. short of money) *(B)*

Bal-eared – Deaf *(G)*

Balshag – A raggedy person *(P)*

Bampa – Grandfather

Bampi – Grandfather *(B)*

Bar! – Exclamation

Bara-bit – A small thing, a piece, or crumbs (*bara* is bread in Welsh) *(V)*

Barb – A man's stubbly beard

Bard – Bad or ill *(V)*

Bardd – Professional Welsh bard or poet from antiquity

Barmy – Crazy

Bat and catty – Old children's batting game *(B)*

Beading ceremony – Type of wedding ceremony associated with Gower and Pembroke

Bedgown/Betgwn – Welsh costume's gown

Belfago – Loudly *(V)*

Betingalw – Term for *'thingy'*, from Welsh *(B)*

Bewty – Fine specimen *('ew' not 'byew') (V)*

Big-wallet, a – Wealthy person *(B)*

Blacklead – Pencil *(V)*

Bladdered – Intoxicated *(B)*

Blaggurd(y) – Qualities of a dirty fighter *(V)*

Blonclust – Blow to the ears, from Welsh *(V)*

Blonkers – Sparks *(G)*

Bopa – Aunty

Borrow – Lend. *'Will you borrow me that?'*

Bosh – Sink in the kitchen or bathroom

Bottles – Skin blister

Boyf – Shortening of 'boyfriend' *(B)*

Bracchi's – Italian–Welsh establishment, often a café *(V)*

Brace – Iron spike used in making a straw rope *(B)*

Brammer/Blammer – Fantastic

Brat[1] – Apron worn when cooking

Brat² – The apron worn with the Welsh costume

Brides – Bridal couple (both partners) *(G)*

Brims – Horseflies, from Old Norse *(G)*

Bryn(s) – Hill(s), from Welsh *(B)*

Bull(y) heads – Tadpoles

Bushed – Exhausted from work

Butty/Butt – Friend

Bwci-boo – Ghost or bogeyman, from Welsh *(V)*

Bwrw – To hit something with force, from Welsh *(B)*

Sculpture of
'The Bard'
by William Theed,
1858.
Alamy Stock Images

Cack-handed – Left-handed

Caffled – Tangled or matted hair or fur

Caggy – Stupid

Call over – To begin gossiping *(B)*

Callenig – Gift given on New Year's Day, from Welsh *(V)*

Calves – Trousers or leggings *(B)*

Canting – Gossiping *(V/B)*

Capel – Chapel, from Welsh

Cariad – Endearment term for partner, from Welsh
(W/N/V/B)

Carry claps – To gossip *(V)*

Catamouse – Bats *(P)*

Catchypawl – Tadpoles *(P)*

Cawel – Basket or cage

Cawl – A mess, or a messy situation; a jumble *(V)*

Cha – Name for 'tea', once-term of middle classes

Chairing (of the Bard), the – Declaring a winner
(usually during an eisteddfod)

Chatterpies – Magpies *(G)*

Chesty – Arrogant or boastful, i.e. having a big chest *(V)*

Chochon – Bread bin

Chopse – To gossip, from 'chops' – one's jaw *(V)*

Chopsy – Gossipy, from chopse (to gossip) *(V)*

Chutes, the – Guttering on a house

Chwarae-teg – Literally 'fair play' in Welsh *(V)*

Ciff/Kiff – Sickly. *'He was kiff this morning.' (V)*

Cilbwt – Medical complaint *(V)*

Claggar – Hard rockface, from Welsh clegyr *(G)*

Clanch – To beat or hit

Cleck – To hit, possibly derived from 'to clock' *(B)*

Clecs – Tall tales or gossipy talk *(V)*

Clicks – Child's truce term

Clonc – To gossip *(W)*

Cloncen – Gossiping woman *(W)*

Cob (Cop) – To catch *(V/B)*

Coblynau – Mythological race of mining gnomes

Cochyn – Red-haired person *(V)*

Colley-cows – Dairy cows, from Old Norse *(G)*

Comfies – Comfortable athletic clothing *(B)*

Cooing – Squatting down

Coopy – To squat

Coppish – Trouser flies, derived from 'codpiece' *(V)*

Crachach – Snobs or posh people, from Welsh meaning 'elite' *(V)*

Croodle-down – To squat

Crot of a boy – Runt of the children (*crot* is Welsh for 'small')

Crwth – Welsh medieval stringed instrument

Culm – Grains of coal *(P)*

Cup of tea in hand – To drink tea informally, whilst chatting or working *(V)*

Cutty-emmock – Newt or lizard
Cwm – Valley, from Welsh
Cwtch¹ – Intimate cuddle
Cwtch² – Storage space
Cymraeg – The Welsh language in Welsh, *'language of our people'*
Cymric – Latinised adjective to refer to Welsh topics
Cymru – The Welsh word for Wales, meaning *'fellow country'*
Cymry – The Welsh word for Welshmen, meaning *'fellow countrymen'*
Cythraul – Devil (from old Welsh) *(V)*

Menai suspension bridge in Anglesey, North Wales iStock

D

Dab – Fellow or critter; unfortunate person. *'You poor dab.'*

Dal – To catch, from Welsh *(B)*

Dap[1] – To bounce

Daps[2] **(Dapper)** – PE shoes

Dapes – PE shoes (see also daps) *(B)*

Daro! – Interjection for *'damn it!' (V)*

Del – Endearment term – doll *(B)*

Devil fish – Newts *(B)*

Devil's inch – Wild mint *(B)*

Devil's ring – Brown furry caterpillars *(B)*

Devilweed – Bindweed

Diawl – Devil (From modern Welsh, itself from English *'devil'*), interjection *(V)*

Dicky Show Your Light – Children's hiding game *(V)*

Diddikies/Diddicots – Gypsies or travellers (not Romanies)

Dip – Homemade candle *(G/P)*

Doing my swede(in) – Getting on someone's nerves *(B)*

Doodie-baby – Small child *(B)*

Doss – Brief sleep or nap *(V)*

Dossin(g) – Truanting *(B)*

Dran(g) – Pathway between buildings or hedges *(G)*

Drev(le) – To dribble; also spittle (noun). From Welsh *drefl (V)*

Drive, the – Shortening of *'the bus driver'*
Drouts/Grouts (tea) – Tea dregs
Drover (Porthmon in Welsh) – Mover of livestock, travelling the *'Welshroad'* through England to London
Dubs – Abbreviation of the WC (water closet) *(V)*
Duff – Coal dust *(G)*
Dumbledarey – Cockchafer beetle *(G)*
Duw/jew – Exclamative, for *'God!'*
Dwt – Small thing. *'That ant's dwt.'*

E

Eisht – Be quiet or hush. From Welsh *ust (V)*
Eisteddfod(s) – Festival of arts, common throughout the country
Elligug – Guillemot *(P)*
Emmal – Fire ashes
Englyn – Traditional Welsh short-poem metrical form

F

Fach – endearment term, literally 'small' in Welsh (female) (cf. *bach*)
Fairdoos – Fair dues *(V)*
Family tag/Teulu tag – Children's game (tag variant)
Fell – Used for the verb 'dropped'. *'I fell the book.' (V)*

Filbert/Ffwlbart – Polecat

Fishu – Handkerchief worn with the Welsh costume (Welsh from *fichu*)

Fitchet – Polecat, likely derived from *'filbert'*

Flag – Unreliable person, possibly from *'warning flag'* (V)

Flat-shot – Something which is not up to one's expectations (V)

Flook – Flounder or plaice (G)

Flush – Wealthy, possibly from *'flushes money around'* (B)

Fraith – To be freespoken (G)

Frost candles – Icicles (P)

Frumping – Sulking (V)

Fugare – Evening dress or ball gown (P)

G

Galeeny – Guinea fowl or hen

Gammy – Broken

Gawp – To stare, from East Frisian word *gulpen* (B)

Glawman – Raining (usually a drizzle), from Welsh *glaw mân* (B)

Gloice – Sudden unexpected pang of pain (G)

Gnat's piss – Fine, misty rain (B)

Grain – The sparkle of cleanliness, from Welsh *graen* (V)

Granch(er) – Grandfather (B)

Granny's custard – Clay-like substance found along the southern coasts (G)

16

Grumps – Grandfather *(B)*
Guckoo-shoes – Violet flower *(G)*
Gutse – To greedily guzzle drink
Gwathel – Refuse or old furniture left outside house, from Welsh *(N)*
Gwli – Gully or narrow passage
Gyrrwr – Drover's assistant

Tenby, Pembrokeshire. iStock

H

Haint – Tantrum, from Welsh *(V)*

Haizing – Dancing in a circular motion *(G)*

Head sharang – The boss; *sharang* derives from the Urdu *şerang* (boatswain) *(V)*

Heat-tide – Twilight in evening *(G)*

Heavenly Tongue – A phrase for the Welsh language. Cf. *'The Language of Heaven'*.

Hec – To hop *(V)*

Heiptrw ho! – A call used by a drover

Helly – To cover your head (or potatoes) with a scarf *(G)*

He's got his moss off – Children's phrase for when someone's angry

Hesk/Husk – Cough

Hiraeth – Nostalgia or longing for Wales (or homeland) of the past

Hobbies – Part-time work on the side, often illicit *(B)*

How-be? – Literally *'How are you?'*

Huvves – Flooded cavities formed by ledges of rock overhanging rockpools *(G)*

Hwyl – Good cheer, health, or enthusiasm. From Welsh.

I

I've got cree – A truce term used by children

J

Jackyjumpers/Jacky-longlegs – Daddy long-legs, crane fly

Jangle – To gossip *(N)*

Jawl/Jawch – Devil *(V)*

Jorum – Large quantity of tea (or beer) *(G)*

Joyo – Enjoyment, from Welsh *joio* for enjoy *(V)*

Jugglemire – A quagmire or unstable surface. From Old Norse *(G)*

Keiched/Keetch/Klatch – Coagulated blood; also verb *'to clog' (G)*

Kiddle – Cauldron or pan

Kift – Stupid or awkward

Klems – Crab or lobster's pincers *(G)*

Labbing – Gossiping *(W)*

Labigan – Gossiping woman *(W)*

Ladiwen – Bindweed, from Welsh, literally *'white lady'*

Language of Heaven, the – English phrase for the Welsh language

Larper – Small boy; see also *lumper*

Lathed – Invited, from Anglo-Saxon *lathian* (German *laden*) *(G)*

Launders – Guttering on a house

Learn, to – Verb for *'to teach'*. From Welsh grammar.

Littledwt – Small child *(B)*

Locks/Locksens – Lengthy beard

Lolfa – Living room, lounge or reception area, from Welsh *(B)*

Long-dogs – Athletic individual *(P)*

Looch – Spoon used for porridge

Loose go – Literally *'let go' (V)*

Lorps – Well-worn shoes *(P)*

Lovespoon/Lovers' spoon – Decorative wooden spoon gifted to a romantic partner

Lump – Large quality or quantity. *'That's a lump of a cake.' (V)*

Lumper – A young boy; see also *larper (P)*

M

Made you look, turned you into tattie soup – Variation of children's *'made you look'* song

Mam – Mother

Mamgu – Grandmother

March – Wild celery *(G)*

Messin' – To have fun, or to play a game. From *'messing around'*. *(B)*

Milgi – Greyhound dog, from Welsh

Mitching/mutching – To truant (various forms throughout the valleys)

Mob – Children's game – hide and seek

Morgregs – Ants, from Welsh *morgrug* (itself a plural)

Mun – Endearment term *(V)*

Mundle – Porridge stick

Murfles – Freckles

Caerphilly Castle, South Wales iStock

N

Nad – Dad *(B)*

Nain – Grandmother, from Welsh

Nant – Stream or creek, from Welsh *(B)*

Nash – Tender or delicate, from Flemish nat *(G)*

Never! – Exclamative, for surprise. Short form of *'Well, I never'. (V)*

Nobblin' – Cold

Now jest / Now just – A little while ago (a reverse of *'just now') (V)*

O

Old misery – Moody, bad-tempered person *(B)*

On-trust – Deal between drover and farmer

P

Pais – Petticoat or skirt in the Welsh costume

Pan – Washbasin

Pardo – Great black-backed seagull *(P/G)*

Patblack – Woodlouse (also blackpat)

Pelmin – Rainy day *(G)*

Penbulls/Penbullyheads – Tadpoles (*pen* means head in Welsh). See also Bull(y) heads.

Pentan – Hob or grill, from Welsh

Pibau – Welsh version of bagpipes, first used in the 1300s

Pibgorn – Archaic, medieval Welsh pipe instrument

Picau ar y maen – Alternative name for the Welsh cake, from Welsh *(V)*

Picking rain – Type of light rain *(V)*

Pied – Expression of disgust *(B)*

Pine-end – Gable end of a house *(B/P/V)*

Pitch in – To help yourselves to something

Poining – Troubling, from Welsh *poeni*, to worry, pain or tease *(V)*

Potas maip – Peasant food from droving times: thin soup, often made of turnips

Pot-bara – Bread bin, from Welsh

Prill – Small stream

Proper[1] – Adverb, shortening of *'properly'*. *'Proper nasty'*. *(V)*

Proper[2] – As in *'truly'*. *'I want to proper help.'* *(V)*

Pwp – Unwell; Welshified *'poop'* *(B)*

Pystyll – Natural well or spring *(B)*

Q

Quat/Cwat – To hunch over, to squat *(W/V/B)*

R

Rack – Path
Reasty/Rusty – Rancid or rotten
Rhewi/Rhewwy/Rewwy – Adjective for cold, from Welsh *(B)*
Rhiw – Slope, from Welsh
Robin-(the)-Driver – Gadfly

S

Saint David's Day – Welsh national holiday
Saint Dwynwen's Day – Welsh holiday of romance and love (Welsh: *Dydd Santes Dwynwen*)
Savori fach/Safri fach – The Welsh name for the plant *'winter savory'*, meaning *'small savory'*
Scalps – Blister on the skin
Scram – To scratch hard and deep *(B)*
Scribbux – Small wood or forest *(G)*
Sea parrot – Puffin *(P)*
Seed leaf – Basket (also *seed lip/seed lipe*)
Sgidie/Skiddy – PE shoes, Welsh for shoes *(B)*
Shiggle – to shake, from Welsh *siglo (V)*
Shiggly – Child's seesaw, or swing, from Welsh *siglo*
Shinkin/Shincyn – Tea-broth made with buttery bread *(V)*
Shrimps – Tea dregs
Shwmae – Welsh greeting, popular in the south

Llandudno promenade, North Wales iStock

Shybaby bunting – Variation on *'crybaby bunting'*,
of a mocking nature

Siol fagu – A shawl used for nursing your child

Sket/Sketting – Drizzly kind of rain *(V)*

Sketch – Person who looks untidy or has a bizarre
appearance *(V)*

Skinnies – Leggings, tights or 'skinny' style jeans *(B)*

Slummocky – Sloppy or untidy, in regard to housekeeping

Spag – To scratch someone

Speckles – Freckles

Spence – Cupboard located upstairs

Spleet – Knitting needles *(G)*
Sponar/Sboner – Boyfriend, from Welsh *(V)*
Sprag[1] – To catch
Sprag[2] – To trip over *(V)*
Spreathed – Of hands, to be fissured or cracked
Starved – Very cold
Steaming – Drunk *(B)*
Stean – Earthen or clay breadbin
Storming-(weather) – Raining heavily *(B)*
Summer-spots – Freckles *(B/W/V)*
Swill – To quickly wash your face for refreshment, usually without soap *(V)*
Swindle – Sweepstake or raffle *(V)*

T

Tabor/Tabret – Portable snare drum
Tad-cu/Dad-cu – Grandfather
Tafod teg – Smooth-talker, from Welsh, literally *'fair-tongued'* *(V)*
Tai unnos/Ty Unnos – Shacks erected in a single night, 'one night houses'
Taid – Grandfather, from Welsh
Tamp – To bounce a ball
Tamping[1] – Furious
Tamping[2] – Disgusting *(B)*

Taro – To hit, from Welsh *(B)*

Tatch/Tawch – Unpleasant taste, from Welsh

Tea-lees – Tea dregs

Teafight/bunfight – Free meal or cup of tea, often in a village hall or chapel *(V)*

Tidy – Excellent (much-used word)

Tistytosty – Pine cone *(V/G)*

Togs – General clothes *(B)*

Tollet – Loft or attic, from Welsh

Trwsers – Trousers, from Welsh, pronounced *'troosers' (B)*

Tump/the tumps – Hill

Twmpath – Folk or barn dance, from Welsh

Twp – Stupid, from Welsh

Twtty – To be small. *'That kitten's twtty.'*

Ty Bach – Toilet, from Welsh meaning *'little house'*, for the outhouse

U

Under the Policeman's Arm – Children's game – stuck in the mud *(B)*

V

Vair/Vere – Weasel or stoat, from Old French *(G)*

Vang(ed) – To save or collect water *(G)*

Vit – An attempt *(P/G)*

Wild Welsh ponies in the 'Green Desert' of central Wales iStock

W

Want/Wont – Mole, from Old English

Water trouble – Urinary problems *(V)*

Wejen – Girlfriend, from Welsh

Welsh cape (or mantle) – Cape worn in the Welsh costume

Welsh costume – Traditional costume of Wales, worn by women

Welsh fashion, in the – Nursing an infant by wrapping a shawl around carer and infant *(V)*

Welsh harp, the – Otherwise known as 'the triple harp'

Welsh hat – The stiff, broad, flat-brimmed and the tall crowned hat worn with the Welsh costume

Welsh mobcap – Cotton head cover worn beneath Welsh hat of the Welsh costume

Welsh shawl – The shawl worn with the Welsh costume, of various types

Welshroad – A Welsh drover's road that passed through England (also *Welshway, Welsh-drive, Welsh-ride*)

White Lady – Bindweed

Wincas – Hangnail, loose skin on nail

Y

Yobbo/Iobbo – Delinquent within the community *(B)*

Z

Zemmit – Type of Gower sieve lined with sheepskin *(G)*

> *'If thee cast make a zemmit wi'out acrinkle,*
> *thee't git a husband wi'out a wrinkle'*
>
> **Rhyming proverb for hard work**
> **reaping good rewards**

Welsh English pronunciation and grammar

Illustration of Swansea, 1881 Richard Burton Archives, Swansea University

A nameless dialect

Welsh English? Wenglish? Anglo-Welsh? Cambrian English? A 'Welsh accent'? The English of Wales has, over the last century at least, been branded with many different names, with academics and laymen all weighing in with their opinions. Because of the language scenario in Wales (do you speak Welsh/Cymraeg or English?), people haven't particularly focused on the naming of distinct varieties of English within Wales! The two most common terms are 'Welsh English', and a shortening attributed to John Edwards: 'Wenglish'. It should be noted that Wenglish often refers only to the Valleys dialect, however, and not to English in Wales as a whole.

Points on Welsh English pronunciation

There are a few Welsh English sounds which speakers of other dialects may recognise. In South Wales, it is common to hear that the initial *[h]* sound is dropped. For instance, *'hanging'* or *'house'* can be heard as *'[h]anging* or *'[h]ouse'*. Some words may gain intrusive sounds which you might not expect, like a *[y]* sound at the beginning. For example, the words *'ear'*, *'here'* and *'year'* may all sound the same, pronounced somewhat like *'yur'* (without the *[r]* sound). There are also a few sounds which have, quite understandably, passed into English from Welsh. The Welsh consonant *[ch]*, in a word like *bach* (an endearment term, meaning 'small'), is similar to a Scottish word *'loch'* or the name of the esteemed German composer, JOHANN SEBASTIAN 'BACH'. It is not common in other Englishes, and is often misheard as a *[k]* sound, like in *'back'*.

Another sound borrowed from Welsh is the double L – *[ll]*. If you place your tongue in the position of an L at the roof of your mouth, then force air through your mouth (similar to how you can hold an *[ff]* or *[h]* sound), you can pronounce it!

This sound has been notoriously misheard by English ears throughout the ages. Perhaps the most famous is WILLIAM SHAKESPEARE, who could only hear a *[fl]* sound; that's why in his play *Henry V,* his Welsh captain is called *'Fluellen'*, rather than *'Llewellyn'*. One final sound is *[dd]*, used in a word like *bardd*. Whatever you do, do not attempt to make two *[d]* sounds! Its sound is in fact the same as the one at the beginning of *'that'* or *'the'* – a *'th'* sound.

Grasping Welsh English grammar

The grammar of Welsh English has its own rules, and many of them derive from Welsh *(Cymraeg)*. Quite a well-heard tendency in South Wales is a feature called 'focus fronting', where the valued context of a sentence is placed first. Take, for example, *'quiet, he is'* rather than *'he is quiet'*. Prepositions also like to do interesting things. For example, *'by'* likes to crop up next to *'here'* and *'there'* as in *'by there'*. Another common phrase for *'where is he'* is *'where's he to?'* As for the pronoun *'that'*, well, that likes to be replaced with *'there'* so that we find statements like *'there's nice'* (rather than *'that's nice'*). As the English language has been laid upon the nation, like a tablecloth upon a rustic wooden table, the grooves and knots of the wood beneath remain, and the underlying Welsh grammar can still be clearly seen in the English of this linguistic region.

The World of Welsh English (a brief history)

Anglo-Welsh

What does it mean to be 'Anglo-Welsh'? In essence the term is often used to refer to a hybrid between English and Welsh cultures: the Welsh world viewed through the lens of the English language. The term has been used to refer to a literary tradition of writers who write in English but were born within, or associated with (due to their parentage), the Welsh nation. Anglo-Welsh has also been used as a name of the dialect of English within Wales. The term was first used with such connotations by IDRIS BELL in 1922 and gained wide usage; however, it began to fall out of use around the 1980s. The English dialect is now often referred to as *'Welsh English'* and the literature as *'Welsh writing in English'*.

A mine winding shaft, Llanhilleth
Richard Burton Archives, Swansea University

English within Wales

Welsh English is, quite bizarrely, at the same time one of the oldest and the youngest English dialects in the British Isles. How can this be? Well, English has always had a history within Wales, but until recently was not the dominant language. English was first transported to parts of Wales around the 1100s following the Norman Conquest. As the French-speaking Normans set up Lordship Marches in areas like the borders, Gower and Pembrokeshire, their peasants and the settlers who followed them brought over English and Flemish (two closely related languages at the time). Despite this, Welsh remained the language of Wales for at least seven more centuries, although many Welshmen (especially the Welsh gentry) learned English throughout this time. In 1801 the population of Wales was around 590,000, and of these people 80 per cent spoke Welsh (with 30 per cent being able to also speak some English). However, eventually English gained a strong foothold upon the population's tongues, by persuasion or unfortunately by force (like the Welsh Not, a punishment used on children who spoke Welsh in school in Victorian times). By 1901 Wales's population had skyrocketed to over two million, in part because of the Industrial Revolution and the many English speakers who had emigrated to Wales. Around half of the 1901 population could speak Welsh, of whom 85 per cent could also speak English. In 2016 just under 20 per cent can speak Welsh.

Wales or Cymru?

Wales and Cymru, although both names for the region, are terms that really couldn't be more polarised! In the Welsh language – *Cymraeg* – Cymru means *'land of fellow countrymen'*; in English, however, Wales means *'land of foreigners'*. The term 'Wales' actually derives from *Wealas* or *Walas*, an Anglo-Saxon word that was used to denote things related to foreigners (or the indigenous natives) who had been 'Romanised' in the past (as much of Britain had been). To illustrate this, take for example the walnut: the prefix *wal-* was used by Germanic speakers to illustrate that it was a foreign nut associated with the Romans. Today, both *'Wales'* and *'Cymru'* are used by English speakers within Wales.

Agonising adjectives

There are other adjectives that have been used to refer to things from the region of Wales. Other than 'Welsh', terms such as *North/South-Walian, Cymric, Cambrian* and *Brythonic* have been used to describe Welsh qualities! *Walian* is relatively recent, with the first usage being recorded in 1894. *Cymric* is older and comes from *Cymry* (the Welsh) or *Cymru* (Wales) and was first recorded in 1688. The word *'cymricize'* (to make something Welsh) was first noted in 1888. *Cambrian* was used to refer to a Welshman from 1587 onwards and is a variant of *Cumbria*, a Latinised derivation of *Cymry* (the Welsh people). *Britonnic* and *Brythonic* both hail from *brython* – *'one of the Britons'* (i.e. the original Welsh peoples) – and refer to a branch of Celtic languages (first used in 1879). Occasionally the words *'Celt'* and *'Celtic'* are used to refer to the Welsh world, although this term also applies to other Britons (such as the Cornish) and *Gaels* (Manx, Scottish-Gaelic and Irish) too.

The Whys, Hows and Wheres of some Welsh English vocabulary

'A Welsh accent, there's nice'

In the 21st century, attitudes towards the Welsh accent from those beyond Wales's borders are at an all-time high: it's popular, attractive and some even consider it 'sexy'. In a recent public survey on the most attractive accents of the UK (conducted by internet-based market research firm YouGov), the poll revealed that the British public found that the Welsh English accents were some of the most attractive in the UK, after the Irish accent and received pronunciation (the standard British accent). The popularity of a Welsh accent was followed by those of Yorkshire and the West Country, while the accents of some of the English cities were perceived to be less attractive (such as Birmingham and Liverpool).

Research by linguist Mercedes Durham, conducted

between 2012 and 2013, analysed Twitter posts to see what the internet-using public thought of the accent by looking at what words accompanied the words 'Welsh' and 'accent'. Some 'hated' the accent; some 'loved' the accent. Speaking of her research, Durham states that people were far more likely to find the accent 'sexy' rather than 'ugly'. Some choice tweets include: *'If the Welsh accent was a person we would be dating,'* and *'*welsh accent* 'your voice is well lush',* although one tweet exclaimed: *'Dad said if I ever pick up a Welsh accent I'll be banished from the family.'*

Lost for words? Use a Welsh one!

Despite being close neighbours, the English language has been pretty hesitant in borrowing words from the Welsh language, although a few words have crept in here and there. For example: 'bard' (a poet), 'dad', 'coombe', 'cromlech' and possibly even 'flannel' and 'penguin' all hail from that 'Heavenly Tongue'. Welsh English dialects, understandably, have plenty of loaned words from Welsh. Some of these words aren't directly translatable into English and therefore they illustrate niche concepts that English didn't have words for … but do now! Take for example, *gwathel* (from the Welsh word *gweddil*, meaning remnant): it's a word used specifically for furniture left behind when somebody moves house. Want to use fewer words to describe some vaguely unpleasant taste? Well, then, the Welsh English word *tawch* (or *tatch*) will suffice; it comes from the Welsh word for haziness or fog. Are you pining for a particular homely place – perhaps one that no longer exists other than in your memory? Well, that nostalgic feeling is known as *hiraeth*. Although originally referring to a longing for the Wales of the past, today it is often used to refer to any place or person confined to someone's memory.

Pentre Ifan is a Neolithic cromlech in Pembrokeshire that is at least 5000 years old! iStock

To *cwtsh* or not to *cwtch*?

A much-loved Welsh word used extensively throughout Wales is *cwtch* or *cwtsh*, which is a word for both a snuggly cuddle and for a cosy, hidden place (from dads' sheds to cupboards under the stairs!). Unknown to many, cwtch is actually a much-travelled word. It's only most recently been associated with the Welsh world. It's actually a welshification of the Middle English word *couch*, which came from the French word *coucher*, and even before that the Latin *collocāre*, all of which mean *'to lay something in place'*. Its usage in 21st-century Wales is certainly increasing in popularity and in 2013 it was voted the nation's favourite word. So well loved is the word that in 2005 one wedding couple from Cardiff even changed their wedding vows from *'to love and to hold'* to *'to love and to cwtch!'*

If you walk the streets of Welsh towns and cities today (especially around South Wales), the likelihood is you'll come across a business or two who have adopted the cuddly name into their working lives. A quick glance through the phonebook and a quick tally reveals some interesting usages! Unsurprisingly, at the top of the tally were cafés and coffee shops. Who doesn't love a snuggle with a hot chocolate or cuppa? It would seem the nation's love for *cwtching* their kids comes second, with five crèche and childminding services using the name. Gift shops, clothing stores, beauty salons and pet services also long for a Welsh *cwtch*. It was surprising to find that even legal and advertising consultants embraced the word for their clientele! The power of *The Cwtch* is so far-reaching that it has even wrapped its arms around English settlements too (in Cornwall and London). Who knows, next time you're in Wales, perhaps you'll *'have a cwtch, in the cwtshy corner at The Café Cwtch'*?

From *Caerdydd* with *cariad*

Another much-loved word in Welsh English is, quite aptly, a word meaning love – *cariad*. *Cariad* is often used as a term of endearment. From scouring local business listings throughout Wales, a few patterns have emerged. Unlike *cwtch*, establishments who offer a bit of compassion in their services are those dealing in the business of love. In other words: wedding planners topped the list (we counted eleven!). Cafés, coffee shops, cake makers and even ladies' clothes shops adopted the name too. More curious usages of *cariad* were vehicle rental companies, hypnotherapists and website design companies. Much like *cwtch*, the *cariad* of the Welsh knows no bounds, and has nestled itself in business names in Oxfordshire, Hertfordshire and Shropshire too!

Mitching schoolboys

In the South Welsh valleys, a common word for truanting is *mitching*. It is a word borrowed from the Old French *muchier*, which meant 'to hide', but also to lurk or skulk around; its first use in Welsh English (as well as Irish English and

South-West England English) dates to the 16th century. Much like the children defying school rules, it would seem that the word itself cannot be pinned down and has its own playful tendencies. Although *mitching* and *mutching* (the vowel sounds in 'mitten' /ɪ/ and 'much' /ʌ/) are the common forms, surveys have noted that there are few rules in spelling and pronouncing the word; it truly changes depending on in which valley you've chosen to elude your teachers! Other forms include *murching* (the vowel in 'lurch' /ɜː/), *morching* (the vowel in 'more' /ɔː/) and *mouching* (the vowel in 'mouse' /aʊ/). The form *mutcho* has even arisen, which does away with the -ing ending altogether!

Teachers and schoolchildren in Croespenmaen School
© Amgueddfa Cymru – National Museum Wales

'Merthyr' by Glyn Jones

On that hill, varnished in the glazing tide
Of evening, stand me, with the petrified
Plantations, the long blue spoonful of the lake,
The gold stook-tufted acres without break
Below me, and the distant corduroy
Glass of the river – which, a mitching boy,
I fished – flowing as though to quench
The smouldering coalfield in its open trench
Of steamy valley, fifteen miles away.

(Copyright: Literature Wales)

The chopsy labigan

Anthropologist ROBIN DUNBAR proposes that the human concept of language may not have been created by our stone-age ancestors to fulfil the purpose of coordinating hunts, nor to tell tales about a tribe's supernatural origins, but arose simply to have a good gossip about your neighbour. Having a natter is a popular pastime in Wales as much as anywhere in Britain, so much so that we've coined a shedload of words for the social pastime. In the valleys you'll likely have a *chopse* and will be *chopsing* (derived from *chops*, as in someone's mouth); and, if you've mastered the art, you'll likely tell some *clecs* (gossipy tall stories). To the east, near the border in Monmouthshire, gossiping is known as *canting* and if you want to *cant* you will call over somebody to do so. Whilst in South-West Wales (Dyfed), you'll find yourself having a *clonc*, or perhaps even *labbing*. In Llanelli and Swansea, gossiping's been known as *carry claps*. So gossipy are the ladies along the coast, they've acquired titles such as *cloncen* and *labigan* (both derived from Welsh). In the North-East and North-West of Wales, gossipers are often known as *janglers* because they 'jangle' their mouths!

Steamships at Barry docks, 1908 Richard Burton Archives, Swansea University

The Brittonic Brahma

The South-Eastern Welsh English word *brammer* (also *blemmer* or *blammer*) means 'fantastic' (e.g. *'that's blammer, that is'*) and it has quite a fantastic origin. The word is likely derived from none other than the Hindu god BRAHMA, the god of creation! How did this come to be? A clue lies in another South Welsh English word of Indian origin: *head sharing*, which means 'the boss'. The *sharang* part emerged from the Urdu word *ṣerang* (meaning boatswain). It was in the 19th century that Wales saw sailors from the Indian subcontinent (many of whom worked on British ships) settling in the dock areas of Cardiff and Newport. The likelihood is that these now well-used words hopped the ship with their speakers and settled in valleys. As the Indians *cwtched* themselves into the Welsh life, in no time the words too were readily accepted by the Welsh communities already living there.

The Bracchis of South Wales

Since the 19th century there has been a considerable community of Welsh Italians living and working in the Welsh valleys. Desiring to share their Italian ice cream trade with consumers other than those in London, several families moved from the metropolis to the South Welsh coalfield. It wasn't long before a network of ice cream parlours, cafés and fish and chip shops sprung up throughout Wales. Many of these Italian families were originally from Bardi in the Northern Italian Apennine Mountains; as time passed, the cafés were inherited by shop owners' sons, and before long a true Welsh–Italian identity had blossomed. The majority of the community greatly loved the Italians' trade, so much so that the Italian surname *'Bracchi'* became synonymous with Welsh–Italian parlours in Welsh English dialect! The choice of surname potentially comes from ANGELO BRACCHI, who founded the first café in the Rhondda during the 1890s.

However, not everyone appreciated the immigrant population. As bracchis were open on Sundays, Nonconformist Christians disapproved of their presence within communities, going as far as labelling them the 'Italian Menace'. The Welsh–Italian community suffered a great loss during World War II. When Italian dictator Mussolini declared war on Britain in 1940, Welsh Italians who had not yet secured British citizenship were designated as 'enemy aliens' and sent to concentration camps on the Isle of Man and in Canada. Tragically, fifty Welsh Italians who were being sent to Canada aboard the *Arandora Star* were killed when a German submarine torpedoed the vessel.

Welsh weather

An oft-cited stereotype of Wales is that it *always* rains. There is some truth in this, as the closeness of the mountains to the coast results in drastically different climatic conditions across very short distances. Oh, and of course Swansea is officially the wettest city in Great Britain! However, despite the ever-changing wet weather, the west coast in particular enjoys around 1,700 hours of sunshine every year, with Wales's winter temperatures averaging a warm 10°C and summer temperatures averaging 20°C! That being said, both the Welsh language and English dialects of the nation certainly 'rain' supreme when it comes to talking about wet weather, because both languages have coined a myriad of terms for types of rain!

Sun, sand and surf at Rhossili Bay, Gower
iStock

If the rain is particularly heavy along the borders, speakers may be refer to it as *stormin'-rain*, but if it's a drizzly kind it's *glawman* (this comes from Welsh *glaw mân*); if it's even finer still, like a mist, it can take the alluring title of *gnat's piss*. Over in the valleys light rainfall is called *picking rain* but if it's a denser sort you're dealing with some serious *sket* as it's *sketting*. In Pembrokeshire a sprinkling might be called *skirp* and in Gower a rainy day even has its own title: *pelmin*.

Children's Language

Playground banter

The language of children in Wales has its own history, and the rigorous rules of the playground draw forth unique words. When a child was tired and wants immunity from playing the game, it would be common for them to shout, *'I've got cree'* to ensure a rest. Another truce term, often accompanied with a crossed finger, would be *'clicks'*. When a fellow pupil was acting *'barmy'* and frustrated, a phrase often used was: *'He's got his moss off.'* If you were a shy character on the playground, rather than hearing the colloquialism *'crybaby bunting'* you'd hear calls of *'shybaby bunting'* instead. One children's chant heard in the valleys was: *'Made you look, made you look, turned you into tatie-soup'*, tatie-soup being potato soup.

Children take part in a procession during an Eisteddfod
Alamy Stock Images

Children's games

There were, and hopefully still are, a number of physical games played by Welsh children. A popular one was called *'Under the Policeman's Arm'*, and was a type of tag game. Once tagged, the player had to stand with arms outstretched; a free player would then go under their arm to free them. In other places in the UK this is known as *'Stuck in the Mud'*. Another variant of the game was *'Teulu tag'* (*teulu* is Welsh for family). It's a group version of the tag game, and once tagged you have to tag others to join your *'teulu'* – or family – and hunt down the others until there would be just one lone player left. In the valleys, borders and cities, hide and seek was often known as *mob* while the nocturnal version, which made use of a candle and tin can, was called '*Dicky, Show Your Light*'.

A very popular valleys game in the 1920s was '*Bat and Catty*' (or '*Doggy and Catty*'). The game was played with two sticks: a bat and a catty. The bat was used to strike the end of the catty, which was a short stick. The object of the game was to hit the catty with the bat causing the catty to rise in the air, hitting it as far as possible. You were allowed three attempts to hit the catty. After three, the bat was used to measure the distance. Each length of the bat counted as a run. A team was made of four to six players. When one team was batting the other team was fielding, as in cricket or rounders. Children's playground apparatuses also have interesting names. In Monmouthshire and Newport, the seesaw and the swing have both been known as the *shiggly*; this comes from the Welsh word *siglo*, meaning '*to shake*' or '*to rock*'.

Marbles in Monmouth

In Monmouthshire, there was even a dialectal language for the playing of marbles which was known as '*alleys*'. For instance, the chief and most important marble on the field was called the *taw* or *tall*. When play was stopped in order to remove debris like gravel and twigs from field, the call issued was *'CLEARSIES!'* Then when your chief marble hit another and stayed still, children would cry *'Plonks!'* (this is also found in Leeds, where it's known as *plunk*). A request for a player to move to a better position on the field was called *'roundsies'*. And if you beat the best and proceeded to become an expert player, children in the valleys would call you a *'cleversticks'* or a *'champo'*.

On the Menu

A Cuppa in Cymru

The custom of tea-drinking in Wales is, for the most part, much like the rest of the British Isles. Nonetheless, there are some unique words, phrases, traditions and tales to be told of that fabled *Camellia sinensis* plant upon Welsh soil. Ballads from the 18th century tell that tea-drinking was well established among Welsh ladies, despite its expense, and when tea dropped in price many amusing accolades were written to the much-loved cuppa. During the 19th century teetotallers backed the drinking of tea over alcohol and even held Welsh tea-festivals. However, the fact that milkless tea had an uncanny resemblance to whisky meant many alleged teetotallers smuggled in their favoured alcoholic beverage covertly!

One Welsh language proverb is *'Tri chysir henaint: tân, te a thybaco'*, which some Welsh English speakers translate as: *'There are three comforts of old age: fire, tea and tobacco.'* Another phrase used in Wales is *'to have a cup of tea in hand'*, which means to be drinking tea informally, possibly when *cloncing* (gossiping) or working. There are also many terms used in the making of tea in Wales. *'A cup of cha'* (*chá* is Chinese for tea, with rising intonation), was once used exclusively by the British middle classes but is now more widely used throughout tea-drinking classes today.

The art of making a good cuppa is as vital to the Welsh as it is anyone in Britain, so much so that terms have arisen for wretchedly weak Welsh beverages. Whereas you might feel inclined to sip a cup of *'Arf-brew'* (half-brew), the likelihood is that you'd be less comfortable accepting a weak beverage described as *'dishwater'*, *'swill'* or even *'weasel's water'*. A forgotten tea tradition of Wales is a drink called *shincyn* (or *sincyn*). It was often drunk from a bowl and was composed of tea, milk, sugar, nutmeg and buttery or cheesy bread. *Shincyn* itself is a Welsh form of the name Jenkins (e.g. the preacher SHON SHINCYN), but other than the namesake, little else is known about this tantalising tea custom. However long ago this custom existed, it was likely a time before teabags, a time when tea leaves were brewed in teapots, and a time when such soggy leftover tea dregs had suitable words. Rather than *'tea leaves'* they were *tea-grouts*, *tea-drouts* or *tea-lees*. Occasionally, they were even called *shrimps*. A word which has fallen out of usage in Standard English – *jorum* – which referred to a large drinking bowl or to a 'large quantity' of something – has found usage in Welsh English to describe, quite specifically, a large quantity of brewed tea (or occasionally beer). You might find such a *jorum* of tea at the hustle and bustle of a local village hall or chapel meeting. Such tea-parties, where the tea was often free, have been humorously referred to at times as *teafights* or *bunfights*.

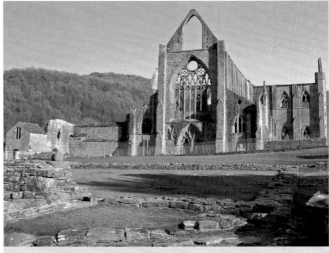

Ruins of Tintern Abbey, Monmouthshire iStock

Welsh cuisine

Bakestone – Term for Welsh cake that notes its cooking method: upon a baking stone.

Bara brith – Type of fruitcake or fruity bread. From Welsh: 'speckled bread'.

Bara a Caws – Bread and cheese. Also used to describe the edible leaves of the hawthorn.

Batch – Small, rounded bread loaf.

Caerphilly (cheese) – Crumbly cheese from Caerphilly, Monmouthshire. Used in 'Glamorgan sausages'.

Cawl – A unique Welsh variety of soup or broth, made with chunky vegetables, meat and the national vegetable – the leek. It's a national dish of Wales.

Crempog – Buttermilk pancakes. Traditionally served on birthdays.

Culf(er) – Slice of bread, usually thick and good for dipping in your *cawl*.

Cwrw – Beer or ale.

Dowset – Curdled milk pudding, similar to bread-and-butter pudding.

Glamorgan sausages – Cheese sausages. Used to be made with Glamorgan cheese (hence the name), but Caerphilly is now used.

Groven – Pork crackling. From Welsh *crofen* meaning crust.

Half 'n' half – A curry dish with half a portion of chips and half rice.

Icelider – Custard slice.

Jibbons – Spring onions. Also *shibwns*.

Laverbread – Pureed seaweed, often served on toast. Welsh actor RICHARD BURTON described it as *'Welshman's caviar'!*

Meth/Mirth – Alcohol made from fermented honey (mead). The Welsh word *meddyglyn* means *'healing liquor'*.

Pant-ysgawn (Cheese) – Cheese made from goats' milk, from Blaenavon, Torfaen.

Pics – Welsh cakes. Shortened from the Welsh *Picau ar y maen*, meaning *'Round cakes on the bakestone'*.

Potch – Mixture of mashed potato and another vegetable (usually swede). Also called *ponjin* and *stomp*.

Tatws Pum Munud – Traditional Welsh stew made with potatoes and vegetables. All ingredients are sliced to lie flat, cooked in a frying pan and served on a deep plate. It means *'Five Minute Potatoes'* in Welsh.

Tintern (cheese) – Cheese from Tintern, Monmouthshire that's flavoured with chives and onions.

Welsh rarebit – Warmed cheese and herbs drizzled upon hot toast.

Y Fenni (Cheese) – Mustard seed and ale cheese from Abergavenny, Monmouthshire.

A bowl of Welsh Cawl iStock

A Nation of Music and Poetry

'The Land of Song'

The notion of Wales being *'The Land of Song'* was first vocalised between 1860 and 1870. The decade saw chapel choirs and singing festivals multiply and the beginnings of the National Eisteddfod. This popular national image is internationally known today with bands like BADFINGER, MANIC STREET PREACHERS and THE JOY FORMIDABLE and singers such as TOM JONES, CERYS MATTHEWS and DUFFY all bearing the nation's musical torch.

Winners: Dowlais Male Voice Society at National Eisteddfod 1903
© Amgueddfa Cymru – National Museum Wales

Male voice choirs

In the 1870s, the singing revolution spurred forth the now-famous Welsh institution: the male voice choir. Influenced by monastic choirs, English catch and glee clubs, and pseudo African-American touring entertainers, the heaving mining valleys resonated with song. The notorious RHONDDA GLEE SOCIETY won a victory at Chicago World's Fair in 1893, whilst the TREORCHY MALE VOICE CHOIR undertook an incredible 50,000 miles worldwide tour in 1908. The competitive nature of the Eisteddfod underpinned this tradition and in many towns supporting your male voice choir was as fundamental as your local football team!

The Eisteddfod

An eisteddfod (which roughly means *'to be seated'* in Welsh) is a Welsh cultural festival and is an opportunity for anyone to perform creative arts. The tradition dates back to medieval Wales with the earliest recorded eisteddfod occurring in 1176. It was held by LORD RHYS AP GRUFFUDD and he pitted bards and poets against each other and then pipers and string-players in a grand musical festival. The process of declaring a winner at an eisteddfod was known as *The Chairing of the Bard*.

Eisteddfods continued for many centuries, but by the 16th century the tradition had withered. It was slowly revived and reinvented from the 18th century onwards as a major arts competition. The 'National Eisteddfod' was established in Merthyr Tydfil in 1880 by HUGH OWEN. The association agreed to hold the annual festival in the North and South of Wales alternatively, and so it has been ever since. The success of the National has secured the tradition in the heart of the Welsh. Today, local eisteddfodau are held in primary schools and within towns and it has migrated to Welsh communities in North America, Australia and Patagonia in Argentina; and cultures from around the globe are also welcomed to Llangollen every year for the highly esteemed International Musical Eisteddfod.

The 'Chairing of the Bard' at an Eisteddfod
© Amgueddfa Cymru – National Museum Wales

Welsh musical instruments

The Welsh harp is both a national symbol and the national instrument of Wales. Unlike continental practice, the Welsh harpists held the harp on the left shoulder and played the treble with their left hand rather than the right. Famous harpists include ROBERT AP HUW (1613), who chronicled many well-known harp songs of the day on paper, and BLIND JOHN PARRY, a triple-harpist (1710–82) who, long before the Welsh rock 'n' roll scene, gigged his harping expertise around Britain! An often neglected instrument is the *crwth*, see photograph on page 71, which was played in Wales during the Middle Ages. It was one of the instruments of the court until the 18th century and has recently seen a revival in folk music. It's an ancient design with a lyre-like frame with particular tuning of its three double courses. A figure from Welsh legend is CRYTHOR DU (or the *Black Crwthist*). In one tale, the *crwthist* is pursued by a pack of hungry wolves in the night. In order to escape, he first attempts a forceful performance, and the wolves back off. However, it's not long until they approach again. This time he plays in a melodious manner with little result. The *crwthist* finally keeps the wolves at bay by playing gently until a search party finds him at dawn.

There were also mouth-blown instruments unique to Wales such as the *pibgorn* and *Welsh bagpipes*. The *pibgorn* is a wooden (or bone) pipe with a cylindrical bore, six finger-holes, a thumb-hole and a single reed. It was especially popular among Anglesey and Pembrokeshire farmers until the 19th century, and successful reconstructions are being made again today. Often thought of as a Scottish instrument, evidence of *Welsh bagpipes*, or *pibau*, being played in Wales stretches from the medieval period until the 19th century. They're mentioned in old law texts and poetry and feature in 15th-century wood carvings in Llaneilian Church, Anglesey. Unlike the Scottish bagpipes, however, there was no standard Welsh *pibau*.

Work in Wales

Down the mines

'Mining canaries' were used to test a mine's air quality
Richard Burton Archives, Swansea University

The South Welsh coalfield is the largest continuous coalfield in Britain, stretching across most of Glamorgan, Monmouthshire and parts of Carmarthenshire, Pembrokeshire and Breconshire. Coal has been mined in

Wales for centuries. Originally small scale and used locally, with the emergence of metal-smelting industries in the 18th century it became an industrial-scale operation. It soon dominated the Welsh economy and from the 1840s onwards the British navy depended on Welsh coal; soon after, foreign trade was booming too. It was a dangerous trade, with more colliery explosions occurring here than anywhere else in Britain, and with roof falls being daily occurrences. It was very labour-intensive work and therefore it attracted many workers from around Europe. Between 1900 and 1910 Wales was the only European country where more people came to live than leave! By 1911 70 per cent of people living in Wales inhabited the mountainous valleys.

Mining was Wales's sole industry and antagonism rose often between mine owners and those working under such dangerous conditions. There were numerous strikes throughout the 20th century, with the trade unions and companies battling it out. The 1960s saw a decline in coal demand, as oil reigned king. And so began the closing of the mines. Within a decade, where there had been 188 pits with 87,000 miners there were then just 51 pits with 35,000 miners. Following the privatisation of the coal-mining industry, coal mining in Wales has become all-but extinct. However, its legacy, culture and language live on today as an important part of Welsh heritage and identity.

Coalfield and industrial words

Colliers hang up their equipment at South Celynen Colliery, 1982
Alamy Stock Images

The following is a select list of words that Welsh miners and industrial workers once used. Some of these would be common in other British coalfields too, especially Northumbrian and Durham collieries. Although Welsh mining is gone, you may still hear some of these words used in new ways throughout Wales.

Backslip – Bottom end of a joint of coal.

Ball of mine – Dangerous piece in the roof that can easily fall.

Banksman – Man controlling the shaft top.

Bap – Short wooden plug fixed in the roof to which lines are hung.

Bond – The cage used to carry miners from surface to pit bottom. This comes from *'bond'* – the tire of a wheel/band or hoop of metal.

Bosh – Trough for horses to drink out of down the mines. Occasionally, watering-bosh.

Bowk – Steel bucket which is large enough to transport two men while shaft is constructed

Bubbles – Small coal which will pass through a screen (known conventionally as *'slack'*).

Bunkers – Steam coal consumed on board ship.

Cleat – Wedge supporting the roof. Used with 'pit-prop'. From Monmouthshire farm terminology.

Collier – Miner who actually works on the coal face.

Dips – Small roads leading to the stalls where the collier will work at the coal seam.

Driftmine – A mine entered down a sloping passage from the side of a valley rather than down a shaft. Many Welsh mines are of this type.

Fare – Standing coal which hasn't been cut.

Farewell rock – Lowest level of rock in a mine, beneath the lowest coal seam.

Gob – Empty space in the rock after coal has been removed.

Headings – Small roads leading to the stalls.

Hitcher – The miner at the pit bottom in charge of loading and unloading cages.

Incline – Narrow passage with a slope. Used as a word

for a sloping lane nowadays.

In-take – Airway along which fresh air is conducted into a mine.

Journey of trams – A number of trams (coal trucks) linked together.

Latches – Points enabling the trams to be switched to different lines.

Loose – Passage blocked with rubble.

Mane and tail – Ropes attached behind and in front of a tram to draw it along.

Onsetter – Miner who controls signals at the pit bottom to the workers of the cage at the top.

Out-by – Passage by which stale air leaves a mine.

Pack – Rough wall to support the roof of a mine and to form a passage for the circulation of air.

Pooking/Pucking – Disturbance in a mine where the floor rises under pressure.

Post and lid – A pit-prop with a timber wedge (see cleat) between the prop and the roof.

Race – To build up coal in a tram until it contains the regulation amount of coal.

Sheaves – The wheels at the pit-head that work the cage.

Sliproute – Narrow passage. Nowadays used to refer to an alleyway short cut.

Smooth, the – The line of face of a 'stall' (a working place in a mine).

Staff at Blaina Ironworks, 1880s
Richard Burton Archives, Swansea University

Snap – Portion of food eaten at pit bottom. (A Common term throughout Britain.)

Tommy box or Snap tin – tin for carrying food underground and designed to keep out coal dust. The tin snapped shut, hence snap.

Snore – Water pump.

Soapstone – A variety of fireclay, sometimes applied to the 'bind' (clay that forms the roof of a mine).

Squeeze, the – Narrow passage. These days, a term for an alleyway between buildings.

Stint – The work given to a miner.

Stone-cog – Thick column of stone/coal to support the roof.

Sump – Underground bulk of water where water collects and is pumped out.

Tommy – Meal taken underground.

Tram – Coal truck.

Up-cast – Air shaft which draws out stale air. See out-by.

Water-balance machine – Device for raising minerals by water power.

Welsh method – A method of *'puddling'* (stirring) the molten iron in ironworks. The invention was enthusiastically adopted by the ironmasters of Merthyr, so that it gained the moniker *'the Welsh method'*.

Coalfield *coblynau*

Welsh mining's long history has spawned many traditions and superstitions. One of the oldest beliefs is that of the *coblynau*, who are a mythological race of gnomes dwelling in the mines and caves of Wales. Like other Welsh fairies (*Tylwyth Teg*), they have not only been blamed for causing mischief, but also thanked for preventing it. In South Wales, miners rarely believed in starting new work towards the end of the week and Fridays were associated with bad luck.

The Morfa Colliery disaster of 1890 claimed 87 lives when an explosion erupted through the mine shafts. Luckily, half the miners stayed home that today, as they believed that an ominous rose scent in the air was connected to what they described as sudden blooming of 'invisible death flowers'. Corpse birds were also associated with foretelling disaster. A robin, dove and pigeon were seen flying away before the Senghenydd Colliery explosion of 1913 that claimed 400 lives.

Artist rendition of 1890's Morfa Colliery disaster

On the farms

Although much of Wales is mountainous, there's also level and fertile land. This terrain has largely influenced farming practices, especially in West Wales, with a pastoral system developing. When autumn ended, the farmer moved his animals to the valley or coast to shelter and would live in the *hendre* (old home). When spring came he'd move the animals to mountainous grazing land and live in the *hafod* (summer home).

Farming words

Bailey – Enclosed yard at back of house *(B)*

Bait – Snacks eaten during farm labour *(B)*

Belg – Bellow *(P)*

Blawb – Clog at the end of a horse's tether securing it to the stall *(B)*

Bwbach – Scarecrow, from Welsh (Literally *'bogey of crows'*) *(V/P/B)*

Bwci bra(i)n – Scarecrow (see above) *(N/W)*

Caib – Double-sided tool for digging and hoeing *(V)*

Cantref – Medieval Welsh land division

Clucky – Of a hen's broodiness *(B)*

Cob – Hair above horse's forelock, from Welsh cobyn *(B/V/N/P)*

Costrel – Barrel for carrying cider to fields *(B)*

Crummy – Infested with lice *(B)*

Daggerty – Mouldy (specifically of wood) *(B)*
Gambo – Wooden cart *(B/V/P)*
Gleiz – Dung used for fuel *(G)*
Hafod – Farmer's summer residence *(W)*
Hendre – Farmer's winter residence *(W)*
Zul – Wooden plough *(G)*
Zummet – Meal to be taken out into the fields *(G)*

Over the Fields

Pen-Y-Fan in the
Brecon Beacons:
the highest peak in
southern Britain
iStock

The tradition of droving cattle over large distances is a significant part of Welsh history. In Wales, drovers were known as *porthmon*, and they would drive cattle from the north-west and south-west through Wales and to English market towns. The tradition is very old, and although it had died out by the 20th century due to the emergence of railway transportation, the *porthmyn* are survived by many fascinating terms and tales. At the beginning of the journey, a *porthmon* and farmer would make an informal (sometimes risky) deal known as 'on-trust'. The farmer would hand the drover the cattle with the expectation that the drover would return to him with payment once the drover had sold the cattle in England.

The roads that drovers wore into the earth gained many names. A common one was *'the Welshroad'*, although others were *'Welshway'*, *'Welsh-drive'* and *'Welsh-ride'*. Drovers were often accompanied by a dog as well as a driver at the back of the herd, called the *gyrrwr*. When travelling, the porthmon had a distinct call that many Welsh and English farmers recognised: *'Heiptrw ho!'*; it rang out to warn farmers up ahead that their cattle could possibly get mixed within the drove if the farmer wasn't careful. Drovers earned little, and a staple food upon returning home was *potas maip*, a thin soup which was often made of turnips.

> ### The Tale of Mr Clough and Carlo
>
> *There was once a drover from Llandrillo by the name of Mr Clough. He often drove with his cherished canine friend, Carlo. After a long drove and a difficult trade, Mr Clough was persuaded to sell his pony to the seller as well as his cattle, and secured plans to travel back to Wales by horse-drawn coach rather than on foot. Unfortunately for Mr Clough, the coach driver wouldn't let little Carlo travel on the coach! Thinking quickly, and knowing Carlo knew the drove very well, Mr Clough fastened the pony's harness to his dog with a note for the inn-keepers along the drove route that they should treat Carlo well. Confident in Carlo, Mr Clough sent him on his way. Mr Clough arrived home and after just one week Carlo arrived back at the homestead, well fed and beaming!*
>
> **(adapted from Hugh Evans, author of Cwm Eithin)**

At the home

The lady's Welsh costume is a symbol of Wales and has been for over 150 years. It consists of the *betgwn* (bedgown), the *pais* (skirt or underskirt), the cape or mantle, a Welsh shawl, the *fishu* (handkerchief), the *brat* (apron) and then the tall, black Welsh hat. It was fashionably worn during the 19th century and around that time there were many variations, with various colours and styles.

A Welsh-costumed lady playing the *crwth*
Alamy Stock Images

It was LADY LLANOVER who helped to standardise the costume and, in a prizewinning essay at the Gwent and Cardiff Eisteddfod of 1834, suggested it should be 'national dress'. Part of the reason it caught on was due to the concerns surrounding Welsh people that their cultural identity was under threat from English migrants seeking work; adopting the costume helped establish a 'visual declaration of identity'. Although Lady Llanover's proposals for a men's version never caught on, the unofficial costume for men became the miners' attire: flat cap, waistcoat, breeches and clogs.

'Welsh fashion' – *siol fagu*

In the South Welsh coalfield work was hard for both the mining men and the home-working women who fed and cared for them. As a result of infant mortality in the valleys, many families had more than six children, and the only rest the mothers usually had was a period following childbirth. Work about the houses and villages had to be done even whilst rearing an infant. One particular way of doing this was by using the *siol fagu* (or nursing shawl) to wrap the child around the mother's body at the hip using a heavy cloth. This tradition came to be known as the 'welsh fashion' of cradling your baby within and beyond Wales.

It wasn't just mothers who wrapped children around them; infants' fathers and even grandfathers would also adopt a nursing shawl if they needed to! This method of keeping your young ones close is mirrored by examples in many pre-industrial cultures throughout history. Quite clearly, this old wisdom remained with the Welsh – it really is the most sensible way of getting work done with a little one. Recently, the idea of 'baby-wearing' has been gaining traction in the western world once more; it may have taken a century, but it's pleasing to see that our 'Welsh fashion' seems to be catching on!

Ruins of Dinas Brân in Llangollen, North Wales iStock

Folk-law and folklore: the *Tŷ Unnos*

Historically, there was a tradition in old Wales called the *Tŷ Unnos*. It was a sort of unspoken law of the people translating as *'house in one night'*. The idea? If someone could build a house between sunset and sunrise, with four walls and smoke soaring from the smokestack, they would then have a right to that particular plot of land. Legend has it that if you then stood at each corner of the house and threw four axes as far as you could in four directions, the marks where they landed detailed the boundaries of your new estate. Although historians doubt this folk-law was ever accepted

73

by landowners, today there are many houses claimed to have been created by the *Tŷ Unnos* method. One such house is *Tŷ Hyll* (The Ugly House), which today houses the Snowdonia Society's offices. Folkloric tales state that the house was built one night by two outlaw brothers in the 1400s, although it's just as likely to have been built at a much later date.

Welsh English phrases

The following is a short list of phrases, expressions and proverbs from throughout Wales.

All of a bodge – Muddle or mess *(B)*

As drunk as owls – Very intoxicated *(G)*

As old as Adda – To be very old (Adda is the Welsh form of the biblical Adam) *(V)*

As tight as a wheel – Drunk *(G)*

Bell on every tooth – Someone who draws attention to themselves (noisy) *(V)*

Brewer's goitre – Beer-belly *(V)*

Candle of the eye – Pupil (of an eye). From Welsh (*cannwyll y llygad*). *(W)*

Chew bread – To know well. *'He used to chew bread for our little uns.' (V)*

Cymru am byth – Patriotic phrase used by English and Welsh. Literally *'Wales forever'*

Down below – Phrase for people living beneath the *'Landsker Line'* in Pembrokeshire *(P)*

Draw (up) a photograph / Pull a photograph – Take a photo (slightly archaic now) *(V/W)*

Fire halfway up the chimney – Having a roaring fire in the fireplace *(V)*

For all the tea in China and all the coal in Wales – At no price *(V)*

Have your cards, to – To be dismissed from a job *(V)*

In a taxi for one – Crazy or mad. *'That bloke's in a taxi one.' (B)*

In the bone – Fundamental quality. Similar to 'at heart'. *'He's good in the bone'*, from Welsh *yn y bon (V)*

Lady-with-a-baby – Pregnant woman *(B)*

Making jolly – To have fun, or to play a game *(B)*

Miss a chalk – To miss an opportunity *(V)*

Now in a minute – Soon, although not immediately *(V)*

Packman's puzzle – Residential area with odd-numbered housing; an area that would be confusing to a *'packman'* (i.e. peddler) *(V)*

Quat the Plim – To cause something to settle. Literally *'to lay the dust'. (G)*

Raise the grease – Thoroughly clean one's clothes *(G)*

The earth has a good heart to care for – When you're deceased and buried, the earth cares for you regardless of your lifestyle *(W)*

Thee woult if thee coult but thee cassn't – Literally *'you would if you could but you can't' (G)*

Tis as tis – Literally *'It is what it is' (G)*

Under the doctor – To be taken ill, under the care of the doctor *(B/V)*

Wash like a rag – To wash well *(V)*

'When the fern is a long as a spoon, 'tis time to rest an hour at noon' – Proverb concerning farmhands resting in summer months (G)

All in a name

Originally, Welshmen used a patronymic naming system. There was no 'family name'; you were given the name of your father by using the prefix *ap* meaning son: for example, RICHARD AP MERYK. Beginning in the 15th century this system was slowly replaced by fixed surnames. Many common Welsh surnames today come from this conversion: AP HOWELL became POWELL, AP RHYS became PRICE. The Welsh also started using anglicised biblical names around this time, with first names like JOHN and DAVID becoming fixed as JONES and DAVIES. So, despite all the JONESES in Wales, one can't claim that any one JONES is biologically related to another, only that a great-great-great-grandfather of theirs favoured the name JOHN!

Speaking of JONESES, did you know that the world record for the largest gathering of people with the same surname was broken in 2006 by 1,224 JONESES at Cardiff's Millennium Centre?

Cardiff Bay, Glamorgan iStock

Bibliography

DAVIES, J., JENKINS, N. and BAINES, M. (eds.) (2008). *The Welsh Academy Encyclopaedia of Wales*. Cardiff: University of Wales Press.

DUNBAR, R. (2004). *Grooming, Gossip and the Evolution of Language*. London: Faber & Faber.

EDWARDS, J. (1985). *Talk Tidy: The Art of Speaking Wenglish*. Cowbridge: D. Brown & Sons Ltd.

EDWARDS, J. (1986). *More Talk Tidy*. Cowbridge: D. Brown & Sons Ltd.

GARLICK, R. and MATHIAS, R. (eds.) (1984). *Anglo-Welsh Poetry*. Bridgend: Poetry Wales Press.

GLADWELL, A.C. (1974). *'Patterns in Distribution: An intensive study of dialect and tradition in rural and industrial Monmouthshire'*. Swansea: Unpublished thesis.

GRESLEY, W.S. (1883). *A Glossary of Terms used in Coal Mining*. London: E. & F.N. Spon.

HUGHES, P.G. (1943). *Wales and the Drovers: The historic background of an epoch*. London: Foyle's Welsh Co. Ltd.

LEWIS, R.E. (2008). *Wenglish*. Tal-y-bont: Y Lolfa.

PARRY, D. (1999). *A Grammar and Glossary of the Conservative Anglo-Welsh Dialects of Rural Wales.* Sheffield: National Centre for English Cultural Tradition.

PENHALLURICK, R. (1994). *Gowerland and its Language.* Frankfurt am Main: Peter Lang.

https://yougov.co.uk/news/2014/12/09/accent-map2/

http://www.cardiff.ac.uk/news/view/69153-love-or-hate-the-welsh-accent

http://news.bbc.co.uk/1/hi/wales/6521971.stm

http://www.archive.org/stream/glossaryoftermsu00gresrich/glossaryoftermsu00gresrich_djvu.txt

http://digidol.llgc.org.uk/METS/XAM00001/ardd?locale=en

http://www.historic-uk.com/HistoryUK/HistoryofWales/Traditions-folklore-of-Wales/

http://news.bbc.co.uk/1/hi/wales/8003390.stm

https://carrymycariad.wordpress.com/2014/10/23/cwtching-up-in-times-gone-by/

Available now from Bradwell Books

Black Country Dialect

Bristol Dialect

Buckinghamshire Dialect

Cockney Dialect

Cornish Dialect

County Durham

Derbyshire Dialect

Devon Dialect

Dorset Dialect

Essex Dialect

Evolving English
WordBank

Glaswegian Dialect

Gloucestershire Dialect

Hampshire Dialect

Kent Dialect

Lancashire Dialect

Leicestershire Dialect

Lincolnshire Dialect

Liverpool Dialect

Manchester Dialect

Newcastle upon Tyne
Dialect

Norfolk Dialect

Nottinghamshire Dialect

Scottish Dialects

Somerset Dialect

Suffolk Dialect

Sussex Dialect

The Lake District Dialect

Warwickshire Dialect

Wiltshire Dialect

Yorkshire Dialect

**See website for
more details:
bradwellbooks.com**